ENFOLDED IN LOVE

ENFOLDED IN LOVE

Daily Readings with Julian of Norwich

Darton, Longman & Todd
London

First published in 1980
Darton, Longman and Todd Ltd
89 Lillie Road
London SW6 1UD

Reprinted 1988 (10th printing)

This translation was made by Members of The Julian
Shrine.
© 1980 The Julian Shrine

ISBN 0 232 51485 2

Printed and bound in Great Britain by
Anchor Brendon Ltd, Tiptree, Essex

CONTENTS

The Lady Julian and Her Cell

On 8 May 1980 Mother Julian was commemorated as a saint for the first time in the Church of England. The Julian Shrine offers this publication to honour the event. It would be impossible within the limits we have set ourselves to give any systematic account of Julian's teaching. Nor is there any need to do so, for Julian's own work is available in various translations; a list will be found near the end of this book. Many readers of these extracts will, no doubt, wish to discover more of the remarkable woman who inspired them, and they will have served one purpose if they take some to their source. Here, however, set out in a form for daily use over one or two months, they are offered mainly as a starting point in the time of prayer. They are intended to be savoured slowly, and in the silence to be allowed to dissolve in the heart. They point to God 'our true foundation', and may help us for a brief period to repose in God, our true rest, to stand in him, our true strength, and to be fundamentally rooted in him, our eternal love.

Of Julian's personal life little is known save what she tells us in her writing, and some fragments of information contained in wills held in the City archive.

Julian was born in 1342, and died, we may gather, well on in the fifteenth century at a considerable age. She was almost certainly educated by the nuns at Carrow, a Benedictine Priory, although she claims to be 'unlettered'. Perhaps by that she simply meant she had little or no knowledge of Latin.

On 8 May 1373 during severe illness, Julian received the series of sixteen 'shewings' of our Lord. She became an anchoress, a woman dedicated to religion, living permanently alone in a cell attached to St Julian's Church in Norwich. Julian almost certainly took her name from the Church which would then have been about four hundred years old.

For twenty years Julian meditated on the visions she had received, and at length she recorded them and their meaning as *The Revelations of Divine Love*. This is the first book known to be written by a woman in English, and is now acknowledged all over the world as one of the great classics of spiritual literature.

Julian insists in her teaching that we should see God primarily as all loving: 'Would'st thou know the Lord's meaning in this thing? Know it well. Love was his meaning.' Through her own sufferings, and the appalling sufferings of her time with all its bewilderment, she fulfilled St Paul's injunction to be 'suffering, yet always rejoicing'. Julian was convinced that 'all shall be well, and all shall be well, and all manner of thing shall be well.'

The Cell we see today is built on its original site marked by two fragments of the old foundation; it is furnished as a chapel. It is a place of pilgrimage for people from all over the world, and its silence still speaks to the hearts of men. If you are able to visit this holy place may it so speak to you, and bring you light, happiness and peace.

The Julian Shrine,
St Julian's Church
c/o All Hallows, Rouen Road
Norwich

NOTE
The readings are arranged under subject headings for daily use over a period of two months. In the first place the book can probably best be taken as a whole in two or three readings, and then, for those who wish to savour it, it can be taken page by page as a basis for meditation and prayer.

God is Over All

The Trinity is God, and God is the Trinity. The Trinity is our maker and keeper. The Trinity is our everlasting lover, our joy and our bliss, through our Lord Jesus Christ.

Lord, you know what I desire, but I desire it only if it is your will that I should have it. If it is not your will, good Lord, do not be displeased, for my will is to do your will.

I desired to suffer with him.

He is our clothing. In his love he wraps and holds us. He enfolds us for love, and he will never let us go.

I saw that he is to us everything that is good.

God's Handmaid

He brought our blessed Lady to my mind. In my mind I saw her as if she breathed—a simple, humble girl, not much more than a child; the age she was when she conceived. God showed me, too, in part, the wisdom and truth of her soul, so that I understood the reverence she felt before God her maker and how she marvelled that he would be born of her—a simple soul that he himself had made. It was this wisdom and this truth in her that showed her the greatness of her maker and the smallness of herself whom he had made. And it was this that made her say so humbly to Gabriel, 'Behold God's handmaid.' By this I know surely that she is higher in worth and grace than anyone that God has made. For no one that is made is above her, except the blessed humanity of Christ.

I trusted God's mercy.

He Keeps All That Is Made

He showed me a little thing, the size of a hazelnut, in the palm of my hand, and it was as round as a ball. I looked at it with my mind's eye and I thought, 'What can this be?' And answer came, 'It is all that is made.' I marvelled that it could last, for I thought it might have crumbled to nothing, it was so small. And the answer came into my mind, 'It lasts and ever shall because God loves it.' And all things have being through the love of God.

In this little thing I saw three truths. The first is that God made it. The second is that God loves it. The third is that God looks after it.

What is he indeed that is maker and lover and keeper? I cannot find words to tell. For until I am one with him I can never have true rest nor peace. I can never know it until I am held so close to him that there is nothing in between.

God, Our True Rest

This is the cause why we are not at rest in heart and soul: that here we seek rest in things that are so little there is no rest in them, and we do not know our God who is all mighty, all wise and all good. For he is true rest.

No soul can have rest until it finds created things are empty. When the soul gives up all for love, so that it can have him that is all, then it finds true rest.

For he is endless and has made us for his own self only, and has restored us by his blessed Passion, and keeps us in his blessed love. And he does all this through his goodness.

God of your goodness give me yourself, for you are enough for me.

Trust, the Highest Prayer

Then the way we often pray came into my mind and how, through lack of knowing and understanding of the ways of love, we pester him with petitions.

Then I saw truly that it gives more praise to God and more delight if we pray steadfast in love, trusting his goodness, clinging to him by grace, than if we ask for everything our thoughts can name.

All our petitions fall short of God and are too small to be worthy of him, and his goodness encompasses all that we can think to ask.

The best prayer is to rest in the goodness of God knowing that that goodness can reach right down to our lowest depths of need.

Enfolded in God

 We pray to God because of his holy body and precious blood, his blessed Passion, and his most dear death and wounds.

As the body is clad in clothes, and the flesh in the skin, and the bones in the flesh, and the heart in the whole, so are we clothed, body and soul, in the goodness of God and enfolded in it.

Our lover desires that our soul should cling to him with all its might, and that we should ever hold fast to his goodness. For this above all else pleases God and strengthens the soul.

He who made man for love, will by that same love restore him to his former blessedness—and yet more.

The Limitless Love of God

The love that God most high has for our soul is so great that it surpasses understanding.

No created being can comprehend how much, and how sweetly, and how tenderly our maker loves us.

Our in-born will is to have God, and the good-will of God is to have us.

There is no end to our willing and longing until we know God in the fullness of joy. Then our desire is filled.

He wills that our occupation shall be in striving to know and love him until we are made whole in heaven.

Our life is grounded in faith, with hope and love besides.

Joy in God Our Maker

 Our Lord showed me our Lady, Saint Mary, to teach us this: that it was the wisdom and truth in her, when she beheld her maker, that enabled her to know him as so great, so holy, so mighty, and so good. His greatness and his nobleness overwhelmed her. She saw herself so little and low, so simple and poor compared with God that she was filled with humility. And so from this humble state she was lifted up to grace and all manner of virtues, and stands above all.

This above all causes the soul to seem small in its own sight: to see and love its maker. And this is what fills it with reverence and humility, and with generous love to our fellow-Christians.

The seeking, with faith, hope and love, pleases our Lord, and the finding pleases the soul and fills it with joy.

God So Loved . . .

 I saw the red blood trickle down from under the garland, hot and fresh and plentiful, as it did at the time of his Passion when the crown of thorns was pressed into his blessed head—he who was both God and man and who suffered for me. And I knew in my heart that he showed me this himself without any go-between.

And while I saw the blood flow from his head I never ceased from saying, 'Blessed be the Lord.'

In all this I was greatly stirred in love for all my fellow-Christians, for I wanted them to know and see what I saw so that it would comfort them. For this sight was shown for all the world.

As I see it, God is all that is good, has made all that is made, and loves all he has made. So he who loves all his fellow-Christians for God's sake, loves all that is made.

The Hope of Salvation

My mind was lifted up to heaven and I saw our Lord as a lord in his own house where he had called his much-loved friends and servants to a banquet. I saw that the Lord did not sit in one place but ranged throughout the house, filling it with joy and gladness.

Completely relaxed and courteous, he was himself the happiness and peace of his dear friends, his beautiful face radiating measureless love like a marvellous symphony; and it was that wonderful face shining with the beauty of God that filled that heavenly place with joy and light.

If I look at myself I am nothing. But if I look at us all I am hopeful; for I see the unity of love among all my fellow-Christians. In this unity lies our salvation.

Because of these revelations I am not good, but only if I love God better. If you love God better than I do, by that much you are better than I.

See I Am God

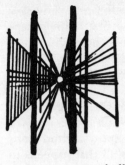

God is the still point at the centre.

There is no doer but he.

All this he showed me with great joy, saying, 'See, I am God. See I am in all things. See, I do all things. See, I never take my hands off my work, nor ever shall, through all eternity. See, I lead all things to the end I have prepared for them. I do this by the same wisdom and love and power through which I made them. How can anything be done that is not well done?'

God wants us to know that he keeps us safe through good and ill.

We shall see God face to face, simply and wholly.

The Far-Sighted Wisdom of God

I saw in truth that God does all things, however small they may be. And I saw that nothing happens by chance, but by the far-sighted wisdom of God. If it seems like chance to us, it is because we are blind and blinkered.

The things planned before the world began come upon us suddenly, so that in our blindness we say that they are chance. But God knows better. Constantly and lovingly he brings all that happens to its best end.

All that is done is well done, for it is done by God.

When a soul holds on to God in trust—whether in seeking him or contemplating him—this is the highest worship it can bring.

The Joy That Never Ends

We are his joy, his reward, his glory, his crown.

For his soul's health a man is sometimes left on his own; but his sin is not always the cause.

Bliss is lasting; pain is passing . . . It is not God's will that we should linger over pain, but that we should pass over it quickly to find joy that lasts and never ends.

It is God's will that we should rejoice with him in our salvation, and that we should be cheered and strengthened by it. He wants our soul to delight in its salvation, through his grace. For we are the apple of his eye. He delights in us for ever as we shall in him, by his grace.

It Is I That Am All

All that our Lord does is right, and all that he allows is praiseworthy . . . Everything that is good is done by our Lord, and everything that is evil is done under his sufferance.

I do not say that evil is praiseworthy but that our Lord's allowing it is praiseworthy. In this his goodness shall be known for ever; by his loving-kindness and by the power of his mercy and grace.

A cheerful giver does not count the cost of what he gives. His heart is set on pleasing and cheering him to whom the gift is given.

And again and again Jesus said: 'It is I; it is I. It is I that am highest; it is I that you love; it is I you enjoy; it is I that you serve. It is I that you long for; it is I that you desire; it is I that you mean. It is I that am all. It is I that holy Church preaches and teaches. It is I that showed myself here to you.'

All Shall Be Well

Because of our good Lord's tender love to all those who shall be saved, he quickly comforts them, saying, 'The cause of all this pain is sin. But all shall be well, and all shall be well, and all manner of thing shall be well.' These words were said so kindly and without a hint of blame to me or to any who shall be saved. So how unjust it would be for me to blame God for allowing my sin when he does not blame me for falling into it.

In these words I saw the deep, high mystery of God which he will show to us in heaven. Then we shall understand why he allowed sin to be. And in knowing this we shall have endless joy in God.

The saints in heaven turn their will away from everything except what God would have them know . . . And this should be our will, too.

Raised by God's Mercy

Mercy is a work which springs from the goodness of God, and it will continue to work until sin is no longer allowed to molest faithful souls. When sin no longer has licence, then the work of mercy will cease. Then shall every soul be gathered into goodness and rest there for ever.

Under his watchfulness we fall; by his blessed love and strength and wisdom we are defended; and through mercy and through grace we are lifted up to many joys.

Whenever we contemplate what is forbidden, our Lord touches us tenderly and calls us kindly, saying to our soul, 'Forget this fancy. Turn to me. I am enough for you. Rejoice in your saviour and your salvation.'

This is our Lord's will: that we trust him and search for him, enjoy him and delight in him, and comfort and strengthen ourselves, as by his help and grace we may, until such time as we see him face to face.

Yearning for God

By repentance we are made clean; by compassion we are made ready; and by yearning for God we are made worthy.

Though the soul's wounds heal, the scars remain. God sees them not as blemishes but as honours.

Peace and love are always alive in us, but we are not always alive to peace and love.

I know full well that the more the soul sees of God, the more it desires him, by his grace.

I had no liking for any other heaven than Jesus, who will be my joy when I come there.

Sin Cannot Hinder Love

Full lovingly does our Lord hold us when it seems to us we are nearly forsaken and cast away because of our sin—and deservedly so.

Our courteous Lord does not want his servants to despair even when they fall often and grievously into sin. For our falling does not hinder him from loving us.

This is princely friendship from our courteous Lord that he still sustains us secretly even while we are in sin. He touches us gently and shows us our sin by the kindly light of mercy and grace.

His will is that we should be like him in wholeness and never-ending love to ourselves and our fellow-Christians.

The Ground of Our Praying

Prayer is the deliberate and persevering action of the soul. It is true and enduring, and full of grace. Prayer fastens the soul to God and makes it one with his will, through the deep inward working of the Holy Spirit.

I am the ground of your praying. First, it is my will that you should have this; then I make it your will, too; then I make you ask for it, and you do so. How then should you not have what you pray for?

Everything our good Lord makes us to pray for, he has ordained that we should have since before time began.

When we come to heaven, our prayers shall be waiting for us as part of our delight, with endless joyful thanks from God.

Perseverance in Prayer

Our prayer brings great joy and gladness to our Lord. He wants it and awaits it.

By his grace he can make us as like him in inward being as we are in outward form. This is his blessed will.

So he says this, 'Pray inwardly, even though you find no joy in it. For it does good, though you feel nothing, see nothing, yes, even though you think you cannot pray. For when you are dry and empty, sick and weak, your prayers please me, though there be little enough to please you. All believing prayer is precious to me.'

God accepts the good-will and work of his servants, no matter how we feel.

Thankfulness from the Heart

It pleases God that by the help of his grace we should work away at our praying and our living, directing all our powers to him until in the fullness of joy we have him whom we seek—Jesus.

Thankfulness and prayer belong together. Thanksgiving is the deep inward certainty which moves us with reverent and loving fear to turn with all our strength to the work to which God stirs us, giving thanks and praise from the depths of our hearts.

Sometimes thanksgiving overflows into words and says, 'Good Lord, I thank you. Blessed be your name.' And sometimes when our hearts are dry and without feeling, or when we are assaulted by temptation, then we are driven by reason and grace to call upon our Lord with our voice, rehearsing his blessed Passion and great goodness.

The simple enjoyment of our Lord is in itself a most blessed form of thanksgiving. This is so in his sight.

Waiting upon God

 This is our Lord's will: that our prayer and our trust should be equally generous. For if our trust is not as generous as our prayer we cannot worship God to the full, and we hinder and harm ourselves.

Sometimes it seems that we have been praying a long time and still do not have what we ask. But we should not be sad. I am sure that what our Lord means is that either we should wait for a better time, or more grace, or a better gift.

This is his meaning: that we should see what he does, and pray that it should be done. One is not enough without the other.

It is our Lord's will that, whatever he plans to do, we should pray for it, either in particular or in general. The joy and delight it gives him, and the thanks and glory we shall be given because of it, pass all understanding—in my sight.

Drawn to Him by Love

If we do what we can, and ask in truth for mercy and grace, then all we lack we shall find in him.

I am sure that no one can ask for mercy and grace with his whole heart, unless mercy and grace have already been given to him.

Prayer is the proper understanding of the fullness of joy that is to be; an understanding which comes from deep desire and sure trust.

We follow him and he draws us to himself by love. For I saw and understood that his great overflowing goodness fulfills all our gifts.

Prayer makes the soul one with God.

Wondering Delight in God

I saw, too, that his unceasing work in every thing is done so well, so wisely, and so mightily that it is beyond our power to imagine, guess, or think.

When by his grace our courteous Lord shows himself to our soul, then we have what we desire and for the time we see nothing more to pray for, but all our mind and strength is gathered up in the sight of him. This is a high, unimaginable prayer in my sight.

Truth sees God, wisdom beholds God and from these two comes a third, a holy wondering delight in God, which is love. Where there is truth and wisdom there also is true love, springing from them both.

When we die we shall come to God knowing ourselves clearly, having God wholly. We shall be enfolded in God for ever, seeing him truly, feeling him fully, hearing him spiritually, smelling him delectably, and tasting him sweetly.

God Is Our Peace

The soul is immediately at one with God, when it is truly at peace in itself.

God is our sure rock, and he shall be our whole joy and make us as changeless as he is, when we reach the heavens.

When we come to receive the reward that grace has won for us, then we shall thank and bless our Lord, for ever rejoicing that we were called upon to suffer.

I saw full surely that wherever our Lord appears, peace reigns, and anger has no place. For I saw no whit of anger in God—in short or in long term.

It is God's will that we should serve him steadfastly for love, without grumbling or striving against him, until our life's end.

We Are His Crown

 Although, because of our anger and wilfulness, we are now in trouble, sadness and distress, as happens to those who stumble and are blind, we are still kept safe and sound in God's merciful keeping so that we are not lost.

Because of the storms and sorrows that beset us here we often seem to be dead in spirit—as men judge. But in the sight of God, no soul that shall be saved is ever dead, nor ever shall be.

I saw that God is our true peace. He watches over us when we can find no rest, and he works continually to bring us to peace that shall never end.

We are his crown, and this crown is the joy of the Father, the glory of the Son, and the happiness of the Holy Spirit, and the endless wondering delight of all who are in heaven.

The Servant's Willingness

I saw two persons in bodily form: a lord and a
servant. . . . The lord is seated in solemn state, at
rest and in peace. The servant is standing by his
lord respectfully, ready to do his master's will.
With love, gracious and tender, the lord looks
upon his servant, and sends him on an errand to
a certain place. Not only does the servant go, but
he darts off at once, running at great speed, for
love's sake, to do his master's bidding. Almost at
once he falls into a ditch and hurts himself badly.
He moans and groans, cries out and struggles, but
he cannot get up or help himself in any way. Yet,
as I saw it, his greatest trial was that there was no
comfort at hand; for he was unable so much as to
turn his face to look upon his loving lord, in
whom is full comfort; and this, although he was
very close to him. Instead, behaving weakly and
foolishly for the time being, he thought only of
his grief and distress.

The Servant's Suffering

In his plight he suffered seven great pains. First, there was the severe bruising from the fall, and this hurt him greatly; secondly, there was the sheer weight of his body; thirdly, there was the weakness which followed from these two; then fourthly, he was severely shocked and stunned, so that he had almost forgotten his own love; in the fifth place, he was unable to get up. The sixth pain was to me extraordinary, for this was that he lay all alone. I looked and searched all round, but far or near, high or low, I could see no one to help him. And the last pain was that he lay in a lonely place, narrow, rough and forbidding.

I marvelled how this servant could meekly suffer such distress, and I looked carefully to see if I could discover any fault in him, or if his master should assign any blame. But I saw none: for the only cause of his fall was his good-will and his eagerness. He was now in spirit just as willing and good as when he had stood before his lord ready to do his will.

The Lord's Courtesy

His loving lord, now tenderly looking upon his servant, regards him in two ways. First, outwardly, very lovingly and gently, with great compassion and pity . . . Then, secondly . . . I saw the lord greatly rejoicing in the thought of the deserved rest and high honour he will surely bestow on his servant by his bounteous grace . . . It was as though this courteous lord had said, 'See my beloved servant here, what hurt and distress he has endured in service for love of me—and of his good-will. Is it not fitting that I should reward him for his fright and fear, his pain and his wounds, and all his grief? And not only this. Should I not award him a gift which would serve him better, and be more excellent than his own health would have been? Surely, it would be ungracious not to do this.' . . . I saw that it must indeed be by virtue of his lord's great worth and goodness, that his beloved servant, whom he loves so dearly, should be truly and happily rewarded, beyond all that would have been if he had not fallen. Yes, and yet more, that his falling, and his grief which he has taken upon himself, should be turned into surpassing glory and endless joy.

The Servant's Will Is Kept Constant

I understood that the lord who sat in stately rest and peace was God. The servant . . . was Adam; thus one man was shown as falling at a particular time, to make it clear how God regards all men and their falling. For in the sight of God all men stand for one man, for one Man stands for all men. This man was hurt in the day of his strength and made very weak; and he was stunned in his mind so that he looked away from his lord. But his will was kept constant in God's sight; for I saw the lord commend and approve his will, but he, himself, was hindered and blinded from knowing his own will; and this causes him great sorrow and grief; for neither does he see clearly his loving lord, who is to him so gentle and humble, nor does he see truly what he is in himself in the sight of his gracious lord. And I know well that when these two things are wisely and truly seen, we shall have rest and peace in part in this life, and by his bounteous grace, the fullness of joy in heaven.

. . . Then I saw that pain alone blames and punishes, and that our courteous Lord comforts and succours, ever being gladness and joy to the soul, loving and longing to bring us to his own blessedness.

The Lord's Compassion

The place where the lord sat was simple, on waste and barren ground, alone in a desert place. His clothing was ample and flowing as belongs to a lord, its colour azure blue, soft and pleasing. His countenance was merciful, his face finely featured, of colour olive brown, his eyes dark, soft and peaceful, filled with deep and tender compassion, and revealing him to be in himself a sure and ample refuge, embracing the fullness of heaven. As for the gracious look continually bestowed upon his servant—and especially in his falling—it seemed to me it could melt our hearts for love, and break them for joy. And in his lovely gaze there was a blend of qualities beautiful to see—on the one hand compassion and pity, on the other blessedness and joy. The joy and blessedness surpassed the compassion and pity as heaven surpasses earth; the pity belongs to the earth, and the blessedness to heaven.

We Shall Never Be Lost

I saw that God never began to love mankind. For just as man is destined to come to endless joy, and so crown God's delight in his work, so man in God's thought has always been known and loved.

From him we come, in him we are enfolded, to him we return.

We shall find in him our whole heaven in everlasting joy—and this by the foreseeing purpose of the blessed Trinity since before time was.

In this endless love man's soul is kept safe as these revelations set out to show. In this endless love we are led and looked after by God and never shall be lost. For he wills that we should know our soul to be alive, and that this life—through his goodness and grace—shall continue in heaven without end; loving him, thanking him, and praising him.

The Soul Is at Home in God

I saw that God rejoices that he is our father, and God rejoices that he is our mother, and God rejoices that he is our very husband, and our soul his beloved wife. And Christ rejoices that he is our brother, and Jesus rejoices that he is our saviour. These are five great joys, as I see it, which he wills us to delight in—praising him, thanking him, loving him and blessing him for ever.

He would have us understand that the noblest thing he ever made is mankind, and that mankind's full and perfect expression is the blessed soul of Christ.

Greatly should we rejoice that God dwells in our soul—and rejoice yet more because our soul dwells in God. Our soul is created to be God's home, and the soul is at home in the uncreated God.

God the Strength of the Soul

We are enfolded in the Father, and we are enfolded in the Son, and we are enfolded in the Holy Spirit. And the Father is enfolded in us, and the Son is enfolded in us, and the Holy Spirit is enfolded in us.

Our soul rests in God its true peace; our soul stands in God its true strength, and is deep-rooted in God for endless love.

And if we in our blindness and weakness should at any time fall . . . we should quickly rise . . . and go at once to God in love; not on the one hand crawling abjectly as if we were in despair, nor, on the other, being over-bold as if we thought it did not matter.

God, Our Father and Mother

As truly as God is our father, so just as truly is he our mother.

In our father, God Almighty, we have our being; in our merciful mother we are remade and restored. Our fragmented lives are knit together and made perfect man. And by giving and yielding ourselves, through grace, to the Holy Spirit we are made whole.

It is I, the strength and goodness of fatherhood. It is I, the wisdom of motherhood. It is I, the light and grace of holy love. It is I, the Trinity, it is I, the unity. I am the sovereign goodness in all things. It is I who teach you to love. It is I who teach you to desire. It is I who am the reward of all true desiring.

Our True Mother, Jesus

A mother's caring is the closest, nearest and surest for it is the truest. This care never might nor could nor should be done fully except by him alone.

As we know, our own mother bore us only into pain and dying. But our true mother Jesus, who is all love, bears us into joy and endless living. Blessed may he be!

A mother feeds her child with her milk, but our beloved mother Jesus feeds us with himself. In tender courtesy he gives us the Blessed Sacrament, the most treasured food of life.

I dare to say full surely, and we should believe it, that there never was so fair a man as he, until his brightness was clouded by trouble and sorrow, Passion and death.

Tested by Falling

And then he allows some of us to fall more severely and distressingly than before—at least that is how we see it. And then it seems to us, who are not always wise, that all we set our hands to is lost. But it is not so. We need to fall, and we need to see that we have done so. For if we never fell we should not know how weak and pitiable we are in ourselves. Nor should we fully know the wonderful love of our maker.

In heaven we shall see truly and everlastingly that we have grievously sinned in this life; notwithstanding we shall see that this in no way diminished his love, nor made us less precious in his sight.

The testing experience of falling will lead us to a deep and wonderful knowledge of the constancy of God's love, which neither can nor will be broken because of sin. To understand this is of great profit.

He Holds Us When We Fall

A mother may sometimes let her child fall and suffer in various ways, so that it may learn by its mistakes. But she will never allow any real harm to come to the child because of her love. And though earthly mothers may not be able to prevent their children from dying, our heavenly mother Jesus will never let us, his children, see death. For he is all might, all wisdom, and all love. Blessed may he be!

When we fall he holds us lovingly, and graciously and swiftly raises us.

In all this work he takes the part of a kind nurse who has no other care but the welfare of her child. It is his responsibility to save us, it is his glory to do it, and it is his will we should know it.

Utterly at home, he lives in us for ever.

We Shall Not Be Overcome

Though we are in such pain, trouble and distress, that it seems to us that we are unable to think of anything except how we are and what we feel, yet as soon as we may, we are to pass lightly over it, and count it as nothing. And why? Because God wills that we should understand that if we know him and love him and reverently fear him, we shall have rest and be at peace. And we shall rejoice in all that he does.

I understood truly that our soul may never find rest in things below, but when it looks through all created things to find its Self, it must never remain gazing on its self, but feast on the sight of God its maker who lives within.

He did not say, 'You shall not be tempest-tossed, you shall not be work-weary, you shall not be discomforted.' But he said, 'You shall not be overcome.' God wants us to heed these words so that we shall always be strong in trust, both in sorrow and in joy.

Bound to Him in Love

 I set my eyes on the same cross that had comforted me before. I set my tongue to speak of Christ's Passion and to recite the creed. I set my heart on God with all my trust and with all my might.

It is God's will that I should see myself as bound to him in love as if all that he has done he has done for me alone. And so should every soul think inwardly of its lover.

He wills that our hearts should be lifted high above the depths of earthly and vain sorrows, and rejoice in him.

He loves us and enjoys us, and so he wills that we love him and enjoy him, and firmly trust him; and all shall be well.

Consolation and Strength

In times of pain and grief he shows us the joy with which he embraced his own Cross and Passion, at the same time helping us to bear our troubles by his blessed strength. And in times of sin his compassion and pity are there to cheer us, powerfully protecting and defending us against all our enemies. These two are the everyday comforts he shows us in this life.

Sometimes a third comfort is mingled with the other two, his blissful joy which is a glimpse of heaven. By the touch of his grace enlightening our hearts and minds, we contemplate God in true faith, hope and love, with contrition and devotion, and he himself fills us with all manner of consolation and strength.

The more clearly the soul sees the blessed face by the grace of loving, the more it longs to see it fully.

Made Strong in Faith

By whatever means he teaches us, his will is that we perceive him wisely, receive him joyfully, and keep ourselves in him faithfully.

Knowing his goodness he wants us always to trust firmly his blessed promise. For in various ways our faith is undermined by our blindness, and by our soul's enemy—within and without.

Our Lord wills us to stay in the Faith. For we are both by his own work and his own goodness to remain in the Faith, and through him allowing the spiritual enemy to try us, to be made strong in faith.

The deepest joy that we can have, as I see it, lies in the courtesy and homeliness of our father who made us, and in our Lord Jesus Christ who is our brother and our saviour.

Full Joy in Him

The greatest blessedness is to know God in the clear light of eternal life—seeing him truly, experiencing him tenderly, possessing him completely in the fullness of joy.

I saw that sin is so contrary to blessedness, that so long as we have anything to do with it, we shall never see clearly the blessed face of our Lord.

He will never have full joy in us until we have full joy in him, truly seeing his lovely blessed face.

I hope that by his grace he will continue to draw our outward appearance more and more into conformity with our inward gladness, making us all one with him and with each other in the true and eternal joy which is Jesus.

Your Face, Lord, Will I Seek

Although our Lord God is with us and dwells in us, holding and enfolding us in tender love, never to leave us; and although he is nearer to us than tongue can tell or heart can think—even so we shall never cease from sighs nor tears, nor yet from yearning, till we come to see clearly his most blessed face. In that lovely sight no grief can live, no blessing fail.

Were we to be in all the pain that heart can think and tongue can tell, if at that time we could see his fair and blessed face, then all this pain could not grieve us.

This blessed sight is the end of all pain to the loving soul, and brings to fulfillment all joy and delight.

He wants us to know that he will come suddenly and joyfully to all who love him.

God's Cure for Our Sins

God showed me that we suffer from two kinds of sickness. One is the impatience or sloth whereby our pains and troubles press heavily upon us; the other is despair and fearfulness. . . . These are the two evils which most trouble and buffet us, as our Lord showed me. And he would have us cured of them.

Our Lord himself gives us great help in curing these sins by showing us his patience in his hard and grievous Passion; and also the joy and delight he had in that Passion, for love. So he shows us by his example that we should bear our pains gladly and wisely. To him this brings great happiness, and to us enduring gain.

He wants us to see and enjoy everything in love.

God Courteously Forgives

Some of us believe that God is all powerful and may do everything; and that he is all wise and can do everything; but as for believing that he is all love and will do everything, there we hold back. In my view nothing hinders God's lovers more than the failure to understand this.

As by his courtesy God forgives our sins when we repent, even so he wills that we should forgive our sin, and so give up our senseless worrying and faithless fear.

Our desire is to fear God reverently, to love him humbly, and to trust him mightily.

If we fall we are to get up quickly; for the worst pain a soul can have is to let sin take it away from God.

The Sins of Others

The soul which would remain in peace when another's sin comes to mind, must fly as from the pains of hell, asking for God's protection and help.

Looking at another's sin clouds the eyes of the soul, hiding for the time being the fair beauty of God— unless we look upon this sinner with contrition with him, compassion on him, and a holy longing to God for him. Otherwise it must harm and disquiet and hinder the soul that looks on these sins.

He who is highest and closest to God may see himself—and needs to do so—as a sinner like me; and I who am the least and lowest who shall be saved, may be comforted with him who is the highest.

I saw that all compassion to one's fellow-Christians, exercised in love, is a mark of Christ's indwelling.

Wisdom and Folly

I have understood two opposites—one is the wisest thing that anyone may do in this life, the other is the most foolish. The wisest thing is for a person to act according to the will and counsel of his greatest friend. This blessed friend is Jesus. It is his will and counsel that we should stay with him, and hold ourselves closely to him for ever, in whatever state we may be; for whether we are clean or foul it is all one to his love.

And then we are made fearful by our enemy and through our own folly and blindness, which say to us, 'You know well that you are a wretch, a sinner and faithless. You do not keep the commandments. You are always promising our Lord you will do better, and, starting right away, you fall into the same sin—especially sloth and wasting time.' For this is the beginning of sin in my sight, particularly for those who have given themselves to serve God by holding his blessed goodness in their hearts.

The Strength of Humility

He says, 'Do not blame yourself too much, think-
ing that your trouble and distress is all your fault.
For it is not my will that you should be unduly
sad and despondent.'

Our enemy tries to depress us by false fears which
he proposes. His intention is to make us so weary
and dejected, that we let the blessed sight of our
everlasting friend slip from our minds.

It is a beautiful humility—brought about by the
grace and mercy of the Holy Spirit—when a sinful
soul willingly and gladly accepts the chastisement
our Lord himself would give us. It will seem light
and easy, if only we will accept contentedly what
he calls upon us to bear.

Holding Fast to God

We must humbly and patiently bear and endure the penance God himself gives us, keeping his blessed Passion in mind. For when we hold his Passion in our minds with pity and love, then we suffer with him, as did his friends that saw it.

Whenever I estrange myself from him by sin or despair or sloth, I leave my Lord to stand alone, as far as in me lies.

Flee to God and we shall be comforted. Touch him and we shall be made clean. Cling to him and we shall be safe and sound from all kinds of danger. For our courteous Lord wills that we should be as at home with him as heart may think or soul may desire.

Our Lord himself is kingly homeliness, as courteous as he is homely.

In Penitence We Are Healed

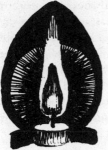

To be like our Lord perfectly is our true salvation and fullest joy. And if we do not know how this may be, we shall ask our Lord and he will teach us. For it is his joy and his glory. Blessed may he be!

In his mercy our Lord shows us our sin and our weakness by the kindly light of himself. For our sin is so vile and so horrible that he, in his courtesy, will not show it to us except by the light of his grace and mercy.

He, in his courtesy, limits the amount we see, for it is so vile and so horrible that we could not bear to see it as it is. And so, by humbly knowing our sins through contrition and grace, we shall be broken from all things that are not like our Lord. Then shall our blessed Saviour wholly heal us and make us one with him.

The greatest worship we can give him is, in penitence, to live gladly and gaily because of his love.

God's Quickening Touch

And when we have fallen, through frailty or blindness, then our courteous Lord touches us, stirs and calls us. And then he wills that we should see our wretchedness and humbly acknowledge it. But it is not his will that we should stay like this, nor does he will that we should busy ourselves too much with self-accusation; nor is it his will that we should despise ourselves. But he wills that we should quickly turn to him.

He is quick to clasp us to himself, for we are his joy and his delight, and he is our salvation and our life.

Wonderful and splendid is the place where the Lord lives. And therefore it is his will that we turn quickly at his gracious touch, rejoicing more in the fullness of his love than sorrowing over our frequent failures.

With Pity Not With Blame

We know by the Faith that God took our nature upon him, and none but him; and furthermore, that Christ accomplished all the work necessary to salvation and none but him.

'I know well that you want to live gladly and joyfully for love of me, bearing all the trials that may come to you. But, since you do not live without sin, you are glad to suffer, for my love, all the tribulation and distress that may come to you. So let it be. But do not be too downcast by the sin that overtakes you against your will.'

I understood that the Lord looks on his servant with pity and not with blame.

In God's sight we do not fall; in our sight we do not stand. As I see it both of these are true. But the deeper insight belongs to God.

The Light Is God, Our Maker

Our faith is a light, the kindly gift of that endless day which is our Father, God. By this light our Mother Christ, and our good Lord the Holy Spirit lead us in this fleeting life.

When the time of trial has passed, suddenly our eyes shall be opened and in the brightness of light we shall see fully. This light is God our maker, and the Holy Spirit in Christ Jesus our Saviour.

'I love you, and you love me, and our love shall never be broken.'

'Thank you for your service and your suffering.'

The Endurance of Love

Though we sin continually he loves us endlessly, and so gently does he show us our sin that we repent of it quietly, turning our mind to the contemplation of his mercy, clinging to his love and goodness, knowing that he is our cure, understanding that we do nothing but sin.

If there be anywhere on earth a lover of God who is always kept safe from falling, I know nothing of it—for it was not shown me. But this was shown: that in falling and rising again we are always held close in one love.

Light is the origin of life; night the origin of pain and grief, the grief by which we gain God's reward and praise.

All Shall Be Charity

I saw and I understood that our faith is our light in darkness, and this light is God, our endless day.

The light is charity, and this light is given us by God's wisdom, according to our need. For the light is not so great that we see the blessed day of heaven now, nor is it denied us; but we are given enough light to live profitably, with labour, deserving the endless glory of God.

Charity keeps us in faith and in hope, and hope leads us on in charity. And in the end all shall be charity.

Charity uncreated is God; charity created is our soul in God; charity given is virtue. This is a gracious gift that works in us so that we love God for himself, and love ourselves in God, and love what God loves for God's sake.

Enthroned in the Soul

He showed himself often as a king, but chiefly in man's soul. Here he has made his resting place and glorious city, a throne from which he will never rise, nor ever leave.

As truly as we shall live eternally in God's joy, praising him and thanking him, so have we been loved and known in God's foreknowledge and purpose from before time began.

Truly there can be no greater joy, as I see it, than that he who is the highest and the most powerful, the noblest and the most worthy, is also the lowest and the most humble, the homeliest and the most courteous; and truly indeed will this marvellous joy be shown us when we meet him.

It Is So and It Is Well

In this love without beginning he made us, in the same love he protects us, and never allows us to be hurt in a way which would lessen our joy.

When judgement is given and we are all brought up above, then we shall see clearly in God the secrets now hidden from us.

In that day not one of us will want to say, 'Lord, if it had been done this way, it would have been well done.' But we shall all say with one voice, 'Lord, blessed may you be. For it is so, and it is well. And now we see truly that all things are done as it was ordained before anything was made.'

Love Was His Meaning

From the time that it was shown I desired often to know what was our Lord's meaning. And fifteen years after and more, I was answered in inward understanding, saying, 'Would you know your Lord's meaning in this? Learn it well. Love was his meaning. Who showed it you? Love. What did he show you? Love. Why did he show you? For love. Hold fast to this, and you shall learn and know more about love, but you will never need to know or understand about anything else for ever and ever.' Thus did I learn that love was our Lord's meaning.

Love Unfolding

And so I saw full surely that before ever God made us, he loved us. And this love was never quenched nor ever shall be. And in this love he has done all his works, and in this love he has made all things profitable to us, and in this love our life is everlasting. In our making we had beginning, but the love in which he made us was in him from without beginning, in which love we have our beginning.

and
All this we shall
see
in GOD,
without
end;
which grant us.
JESUS
Amen.

61

Julian Lives On

The life and activity of such a one as Julian of Norwich does not finish with her death, for the lives of such people create the holy places, remain continual places of God's presence and God's love. Their words come down to us charged with the life and power and the healing of eternity. They pass a judgement on much of what in our age we take for granted. A man's life does not consist in his outer activities, his outward possessions, but in what he is in himself. Lady Julian renounced all opportunities for what we call 'useful work', and so carried on a work of greater value to human life than any other. She did not have the fulfilment of married life, but yet she is mother to an innumerable family. She shut up all her life in the narrowness of one room, but because that room was open to God, the maker and redeemer of all men, she was able to embrace all mankind and the whole world in her thought, in her care and in her love. She had been freed from that prison of self-preoccupation which can follow us wherever we go, however far we go. By her life she tells us that God *is*, and that God is to be worshipped, and that he is the only complete and final end of man. And she tells us that he can be known and loved here in this place and now in this time. By the richness of her writing with its mingling of earth and heaven, of what is holy and what is homely, of grace and nature, she shows us that it is only in and through the light of God that we can ever fully appreciate or enjoy the world which God has made and our own small life within it. For all this we stand with praise and thanksgiving before God himself, to whom she, like all the saints, constantly points us.

(*A. M. Allchin*)

The following two passages are taken from the Plaque in the Lady Julian Cell and the Intercession Card (see the note under Books*).*

The Lady Julian Cell: The Plaque

Dame Julian was called to serve God in the solitary life. From her anchorhold on the site of this chapel she encircled the world by her writings. Her book *The Revelations of Divine Love*, sets out the meaning of the visions she had received on 8 May 1373. From the window of her cell, too, she gave counsel and comfort to the burdened and perplexed.

In this holy place we can almost hear her saying, 'God said not "Thou shalt not be tempested, thou shalt not be afflicted," but "Thou shalt not be overcome." ' Another of her beautiful sayings is, 'Our falling hindereth Him not to love us.' She

63

had found that truly the key to all religious experience is this, 'Love was His meaning.' 'I saw full clearly that 'ere God made us He loved us; which love was never slacked, nor ever shall be. And in this Love our life is everlasting.'

Julian's fourteenth-century world was as marked by aggression, insecurity and change as is ours today. Her most famous words—born of intense personal suffering—'All shall be well, and all manner of thing shall be well'—are as much needed and as true now as when she wrote them.

Go on your way rejoicing, 'live gladly and gaily because of His Love.'

The Lady Julian Cell: The Intercession Card

A simple way of intercession is the way of awareness. *The first step* is to become aware that God has been working long before we came on the scene ourselves, that he is working now, and that our desire is to be linked with him within the communion of saints in this work. *The second step* is to hold the intercession request in our hands and to let all our awareness enter into it. I do not say concentration, as that might suggest a strenuous mental effort and that is not what is required; just awareness as we might stand in the presence of a picture or sunset. *The third step* is to put the slip aside and just *be* in God's presence. We do not now have to reflect that we are there on behalf of another; what has already been done makes that clear. We just *are* in the presence of God, our intention—again we do not have to reflect upon it now—being that God's love shall flow freely in this other, as our hope is, it shall in ourselves.

'Every morning put your mind into your heart and stand in the presence of God all the day long.' All intercession is ultimately gathered up in this saying of an Eastern monk. Bishop Michael Ramsey has written that basically the word intercession ('He ever lives to make intercession for us'— Hebrews 7:25) means not pleading with God, but standing in God's presence on behalf of another.

It can be a help to grasp this. For it follows that to pray for others we do not have to be clever or eloquent or even perceptive of their needs; just ourselves as we are, simple, a bit confused perhaps, but wanting God's will, or wanting to want God's will for ourselves and others. It is God's business to take things on from there. We are to fill the water pots with water—and we are to fill them to the brim—the wine-making is his. We are to remove the stone; 'Lazarus come forth' belongs to him. We are the dry bones; the clothing with flesh, and the breathing upon them is his.

Books

Julian wrote two versions of her *Shewings*, of which the second, *The Revelations of Divine Love* is the more important. It was written twenty years after the first, is about three times the length, and most of the first is incorporated in it. All quotations here are from this second version. There are three known manuscripts of the work: Sloane MSS Nos 2499 and 3705, both of the British Museum; and the Fonds Anglais MS No 40 of the Bibliothèque Nationale, Paris. In making this modern translation we have worked mainly from the Julian of Norwich text of the Exeter Medieval Texts Series (particulars below), which in turn is based on the first of the three manuscripts, Sloane 2499.

The most readily available editions of *The Revelations of Divine Love* in the United Kingdom are as follows:

Julian of Norwich: Revelations of Divine Love. Published in the Penguin Classics series. This is a modern English rendering by Clifton Wolters, who also writes a 34-page introduction.

The Revelations of Divine Love of Julian of Norwich. Published by Anthony Clarke. The spelling is modernized, but where possible the syntax and idiom of the original have been kept. The rendering is by James Walsh, S.J., who also gives a 44-

page introduction.

Julian of Norwich: Showings. Published in *The Classics of Western Spirituality* series, by the Paulist Press, U.S.A., and the S.P.C.K. It is a 'critical edition', i.e. it is a text made from all available sources, manuscript and others. It contains both the shorter and longer versions. The editing and translation into modern English have been done by Edmund Colledge, O.S.A., and James Walsh, S.J., with an introduction of about 100 pages. In a 14-page preface Jean Leclercq, O.S.B., addresses himself to the importance of Julian for today.

Julian of Norwich: A Revelation of Love. Published in the Exeter Medieval English Texts series. University of Exeter. Edited by Marion Glasscoe. The text is in Middle English taken from Sloane MS No 2499, with necessary emendations for the sake of clarity. The editor gives an 11-page introduction. There is a glossary at the end designed to help those who have some grounding in Middle English.

A Shewing of God's Love. This is the shorter version, which is about one-third the length of the whole. It is published by Sheed and Ward in the Spiritual Masters series. It is edited by Maria Reynolds, C.P., who writes a 46-page introduction. The spelling has been modernized, but the original syntax and idiom have been kept, excepting where changes are desirable in the interests of clarity.

Small books on Julian which can be supplied by the Julian Shrine (c/o All Hallows, Rouen Road, Norwich) are as follows:

Influences in the Revelations of Julian of Norwich. By Sister Anna Maria Reynolds, C.P. In addition to what the title describes, there is a list of 'Juliana' comprising about 50 titles, some of which are out of print, and are perhaps available only through libraries.

Julian of Norwich. By Alan Webster and Sister Wendy, C.A.H.

Mind out of Time. A one-act play on Julian by Sheila Upjohn. There are six characters, and the play acts within the hour. Price 90p, post free. There is also a cassette recording of the play done by the Norwich cast.

Julian of Norwich. Four studies by Sisters of the Love of God, and A. M. Allchin. Published by the S.L.G. Press, Fairacres, Oxford.

Intercession cards bearing the words shown on an earlier page. On the reverse is a wood engraving of the Julian Cell by Cordelia Jones. Also cards bearing the wording on the plaque in calligraphic writing. Other cards with various Julian texts are also available.

A leaflet of hymns commemorating Mother Julian.

The Lady Julian Cell Today

Situation The Cell adjoins St Julian's Church, situated off St Julian's Alley, which links King Street with Rouen Road. It lies about half a mile south of Norwich Cathedral.

Purpose The first purpose of the Cell is to be a place of prayer. Each day in the Eucharist and Divine Office worship is offered, and each Friday evening a group meets for silent intercession. Requests for prayer left by visitors to Church and Cell are offered in the silence as constantly as possible. Some like to make the Cell their centre for a Quiet Day or Private Retreat. Guidance can be given if required.

Secondly, we aim to make the Cell a place of counsel where someone is always available, either in the Cell, or in the Church, or at the Convent next door, to share a problem, or to give help and encouragement to those in need.

Our third aim is to be a place of teaching. By means of the Julian Shrine publications on prayer and allied subjects, by instruction, or simply by shared silence, we try to disseminate the sane wisdom of Julian's way of prayer.

Developments It is hoped shortly to convert the vestry into a library, which can also be used as a room for meeting people privately when others are in the Cell. This operation involves the construction of a new vestry in the tower area of the Church. A collection of books reflecting the great spiritual tradition, and reaching out to other faiths would fulfill a real need.

We ask the prayers of any who share our hopes and aims; and if any care to send us requests for prayer we are glad to offer them.

The compilers and translators of this book, together with the cover designer and artist, are closely linked with the Julian Shrine, to which all royalties will be given. If there are some who would like to make a donation, it should be sent to the Rector of St Peter Parmentergate, 10 Norman's Buildings, Rouen Road, Norwich, or to the Chaplain at the Julian Shrine, c/o All Hallows, Rouen Road, Norwich. Cheques should be made payable to the Julian Shrine.

Acknowledgements

The Publishers and the Julian Shrine express their gratitude to the S.L.G. Press, Fairacres, Oxford, and to Canon A. M. Allchin for permission to quote the passage *Julian Lives On* from Canon Allchin's article *Julian of Norwich for Today* in the last of the booklets listed on page 68.

Index of Sources

The translations in this book have been made from Julian of Norwich, *Revelations of Divine Love*, edited by Marian Glasscoe (Exeter Medieval Texts). This index shows the chapter from which each reading is taken. The page reference in this volume is shown in bold and followed by the chapter numbers in the *Revelations*, in the order in which the readings appear on the page. For example, the readings on page 1 of *Enfolded in Love* are taken from Chapters 4, 2, 3, 5 and 5 of the *Revelations*.